better together*

*This book is best read together, grownup and kid.

 akidsco.com

a kids book about

a kids book about ADVERTISING

by Sara Furlong & David Rhodes
OF WHIRLYGIG CREATIVE INC.

a kids book about

Text and design copyright © 2023
by A Kids Book About, Inc.

Copyright is good! It ensures that work like this can exist, and more work in the future can be created.

All rights reserved. No part of this publication may be reproduced, distributed, or transmitted in any form or by any means, including photocopying, recording, other electronic or mechanical methods, without the prior written permission of the publisher, except in the case of brief quotations embodied in critical reviews and certain other noncommercial uses permitted by copyright law. For permission requests, write to the publisher.

A Kids Book About, Kids Are Ready, and the colophon 'a' are trademarks of A Kids Book About, Inc.

Printed in the United States of America.

A Kids Book About books are available online: *akidsco.com*

To share your stories, ask questions, or inquire about bulk purchases (schools, libraries, and nonprofits), please use the following email address: *hello@akidsco.com*

Print ISBN: 978-1-958825-93-8
Ebook ISBN: 978-1-958825-94-5

Designed by Rick DeLucco
Edited by Emma Wolf

Dedicated to happy childhoods
for kids everywhere.

Intro

If you've ever bought something you've seen in an advertisement and either loved it or instantly regretted it, you know the influence of advertising. This book is about helping kids understand the role that advertising plays in their lives and the power they have over it.

Nowadays, ads are everywhere. Our intent isn't to make kids fearful of advertising's sway but rather to teach them how to be savvy media consumers who have the final say in what they want. There is no avoiding ads, but that doesn't mean they need to have control over you. So get ready to say, Wow! Cool! Yay! as we pull back the curtain on advertising to help kids make great choices.

HEY, Y
YEAH

OU! YOU!

We've got something really cool we want to show you.

We're pretty sure you're going to love it...

but it's up to you to decide whether you want it!

Are you curious about what we're talking about?

Does it kind of feel like we're trying to sell you something?

Well...

So, what is advertising?

You may think you know a lot about it already!

But did you know that your
**favorite TV show,
your favorite athlete,
even your favorite superhero**
are all advertising examples too?

Anywhere there's a **logo*** or a product, someone somewhere is trying to sell you something.

*Of course, you already know what a logo is! It's on your soccer ball, your hat, your shoes, at the start of a movie, or that theme park you just visited!

They have something you may be interested in buying, and they'll use people or characters you know and love to get you hooked.

It's important to know that advertisements

AREN'T BAD!

But you have the power to decide when something you see advertised is something you really want.

Let's break it down.

There are **a LOT** of things that go into making an advertisement.

Think of it a little bit like a recipe:

 A JINGLE (A CATCHY SONG THAT GETS STUCK IN YOUR HEAD),

 HIGH ENERGY (THAT FEELING THAT MAKES YOU WANT TO HIGH-FIVE YOUR TV),

 BRIGHT COLORS (BECAUSE THOSE ARE FUN),

 SOME FANTASY (LIKE MOVIE MAGIC, TAKING YOU OUT OF YOUR OWN WORLD AND TRANSPORTING YOU TO A NEW ONE),

 OTHER KIDS HAVING FUN (WHO YOU'D LOVE TO PLAY WITH),

 AND DEMONSTRATION (PERFECT POSES, COOL FLYING, ALWAYS BEING THE WINNER!).

AND ALL OF THIS, COMBINED, HAPPENS IN LESS THAN A MINUTE!

Watching an ad can feel like watching a whole movie.

Every part of an advertisement is intentional.

Each one is trying to grab your attention and keep it.

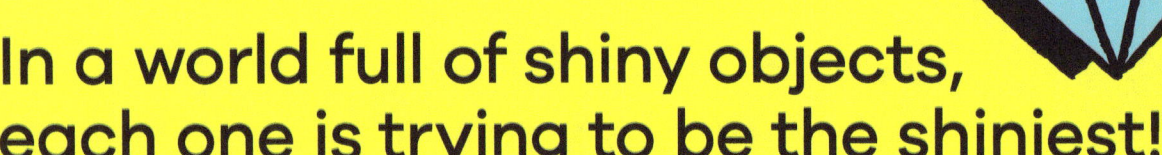

In a world full of shiny objects, each one is trying to be the shiniest!

But it doesn't mean people who create ads can just do whatever they want to be the best.

We use this recipe to make the product look amazing, but we can't lie to you or directly tell you to buy something.

However, there are other media which don't have the same rules, but they're still ads!

For example, think about a TV show you know with cool characters, cars, maybe pets.

A lot of those shows also have real-life toys you can buy to play with.

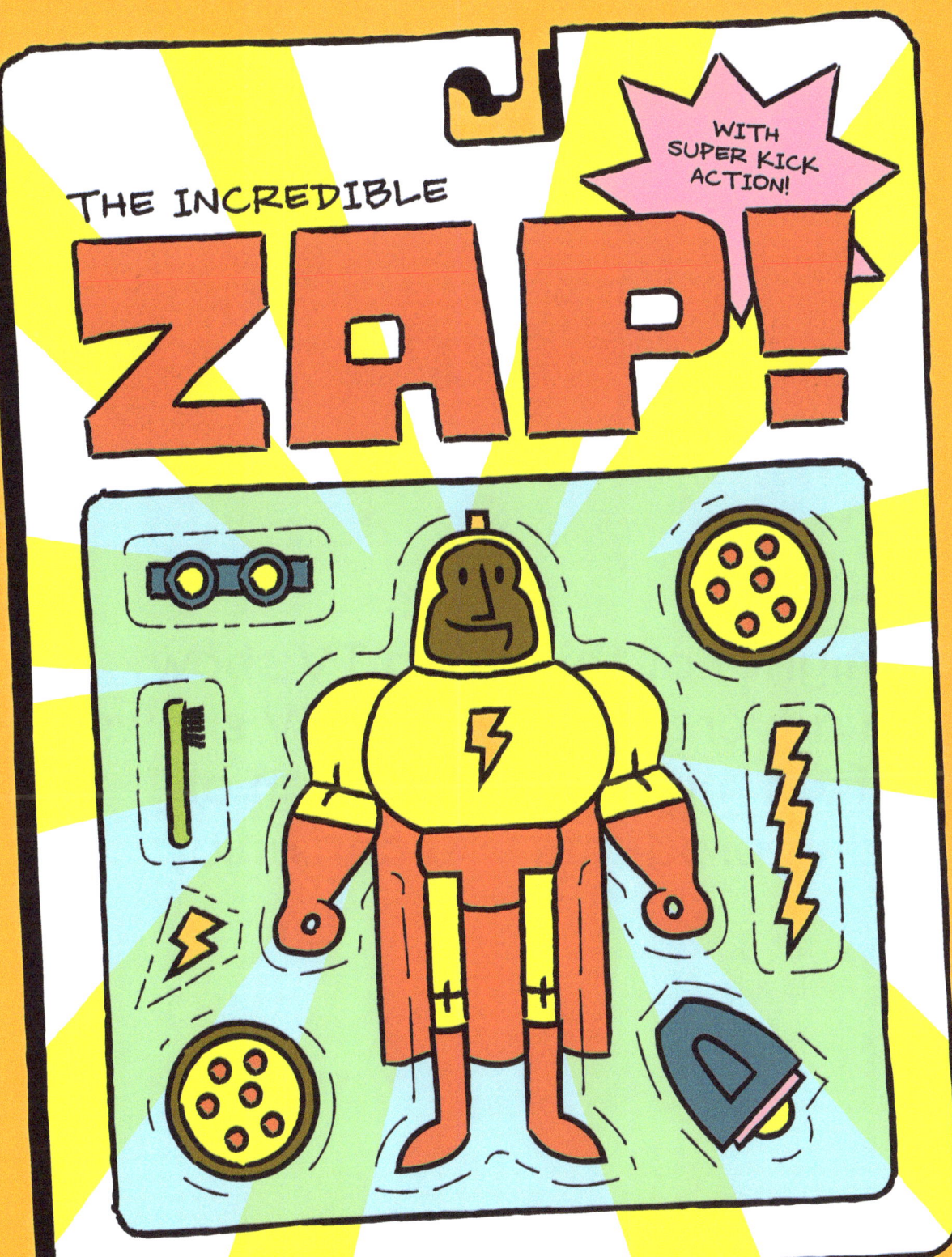

You might not think of a TV show as an advertisement, but TV shows are often made with the plan of creating products you can enjoy.

TV show and movie creators want you to feel so excited about the worlds they create that you need to be a part of them too.

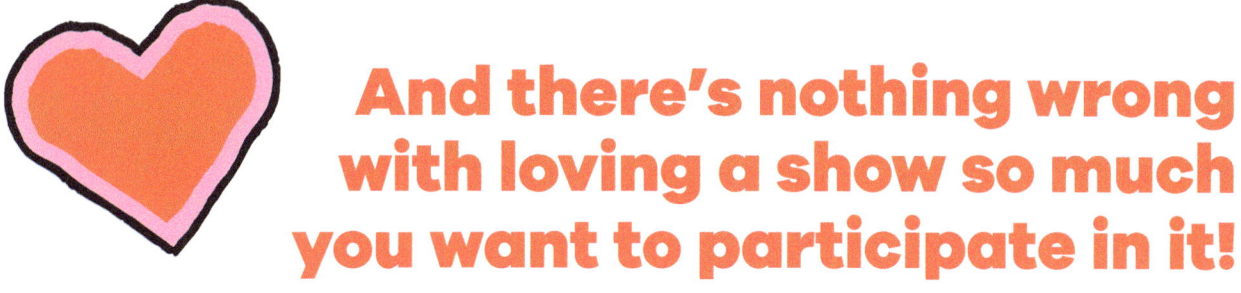

And there's nothing wrong with loving a show so much you want to participate in it!

I bet your grownups had TV shows they loved as kids, too.

 But...you can't be a part of all of them.

So that's the question:

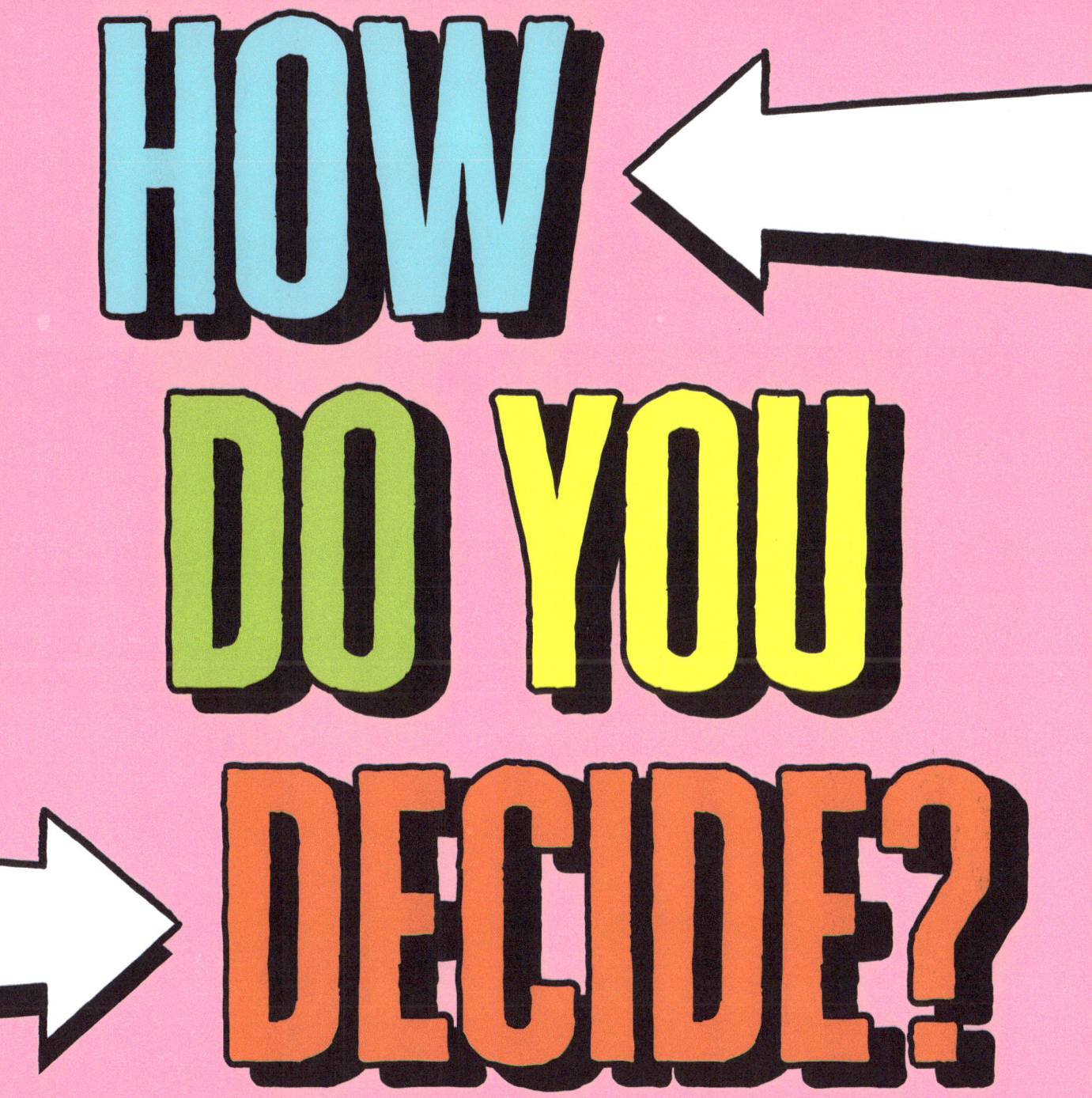

It's important to choose the things that are most exciting to you...

not your neighbor, your sibling, your best friend, or your favorite celebrity.

How do you make those kinds of decisions when it feels like everything around you is yelling, "Pick me!"?

PICK ME! PICK ME! PICK ME! ME! PICK ME!

We know what it feels like to want something that looked so cool, but actually let us down.

PICK ME! PICK ME! ME! PICK ME!

So here are a few questions to ask yourself the next time you think you reeeeally want something:

A good place to start is to ask,

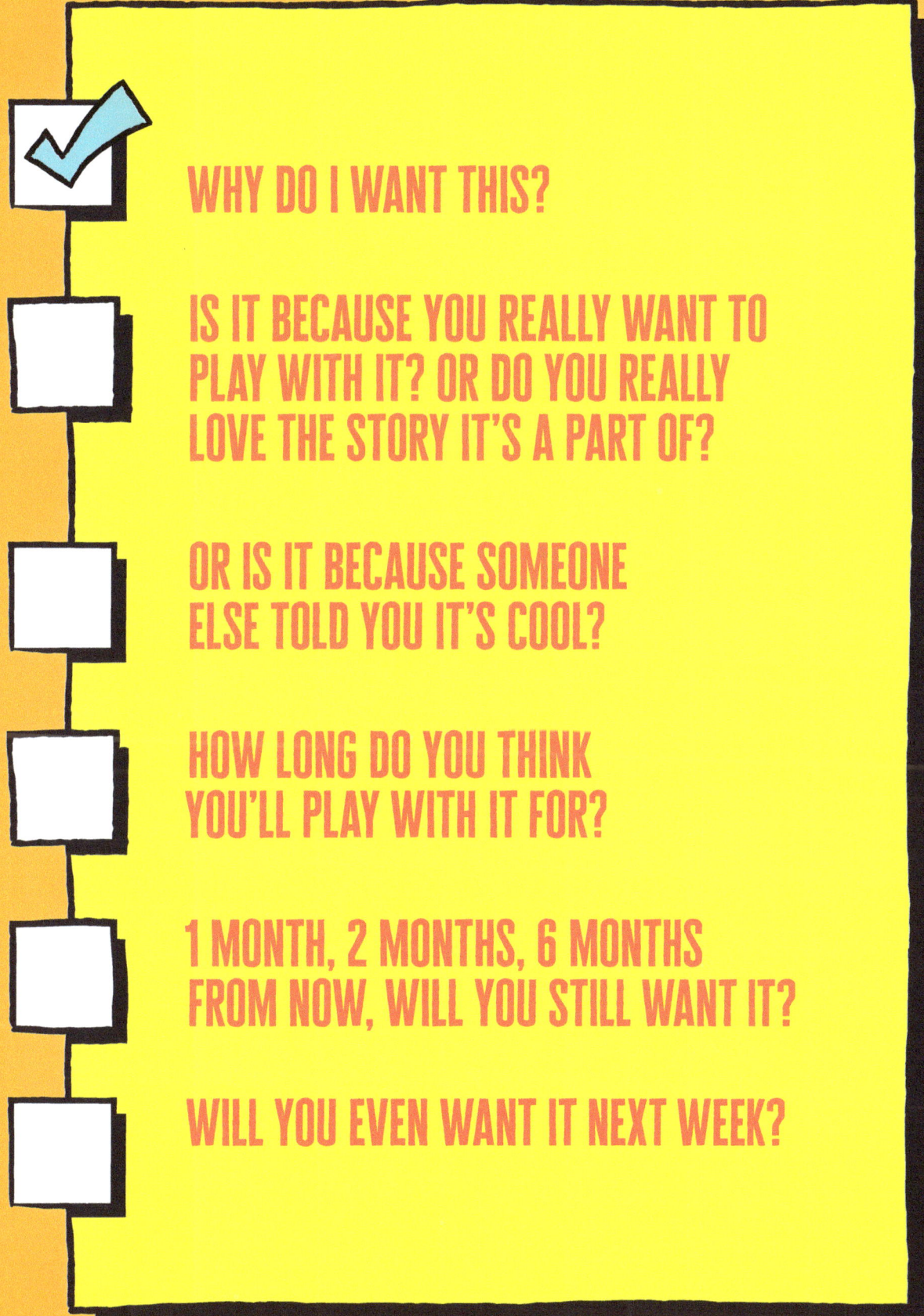

In the last week alone, you probably saw thousands of ads.

Out of all those things, what are the 1 or 2 items that are the most interesting to you?

We're asking all these questions instead of just telling you what to do because we don't know what you want!

Only you can decide that for yourself.

Other peoples' opinions can matter.

AND IT'S NOT BAD TO WANT THINGS!

But ultimately, no matter how flashy and bright and catchy something is, know this:

**If you don't really want it,
you don't have to get it.**

It's always your decision,
and your decisions are powerful.

Supporting the right types
of things can **change our world.**

AND THAT
WITH

STARTS YOU!

Outro

So there you have it! Yes, ads are everywhere, but it's up to you to make your own decisions. Advertisements don't have power unless you give them power.

We hope this book starts a great conversation with the kids in your life about how to be media-savvy consumers who know what they like and what they don't. It's getting harder and harder to protect kids from ads but knowing and understanding everything that makes an ad, how ads work, and what they're trying to do are the first steps in kids becoming more confident in making their own choices.

So, go ahead and let them enjoy media and entertainment, and know you have helped build their skills in making good personal decisions.

About The Author

Sara Furlong (she/her) is a writer, author, and family fun-finder who has been working in advertising for 17 years. There is nothing Sara loves more than creating fun and exciting content that kids love, whether it be in a book, a social media post, or through an ad for the hottest new toy.

David Rhodes (he/him) has been an Art Director and Creative Director in mainstream and kids advertising for over 35 years. In addition, he has been Associate Professor at OCAD University. Over that time, David has seen many changes and evolution in consumer and kids' media. David truly believes that having fun results in happiness.

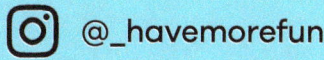 @_havemorefun

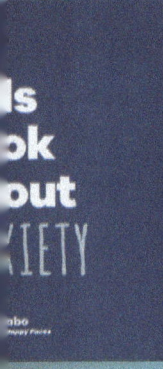    

Discover more at akidsco.com